What Would *Mrs. Claus* Do?

WHERE THERE IS A WISH, THERE IS A WAY

Written by **PAMELA MCCOLL** *and* **LINDSAY STEWART**

"Joy is the gift that comes from making others happy."

- Mrs. Claus

CONTENTS

Introduction: Embrace Mrs. Claus, and the Magic Begins 6

Chapter 1: The Essence of Mrs. Claus 10

Chapter 2: Year-Round Happiness and Joy 24

Chapter 3: You May Be A Mrs. Claus When You… 30

Chapter 4: Mrs. Claus' "Fa-La-La" Philosophy 39

Chapter 5: Christmas Is Coming 54

Chapter 6: I Believe In You 64

Chapter 7: A Time of Caring and Sharing 72

Final Thoughts 89

INTRODUCTION

Embrace Mrs. Claus, and the Magic Begins

The following pages are filled with insightful words of wisdom, direct from Mrs. Claus. Her helpful tips on how to live with the spirit of Christmas in your heart is her special gift to you.

Everyone needs a Mrs. Claus in their corner, cheering them on, offering encouragement along the way. She is not here to "fix" anyone, nor is she able to sweep away problems. She is here to gently guide you toward your North Star. In sharing her "Fa-La-La" Philosophy, Mrs. Claus is optimistic that you will find greater fulfillment with all that you do and gain a fresh perspective on solving challenges. The First Lady of Christmas wishes to remind readers that they are as unique and precious as each snowflake that falls from the sky. Mrs. Claus is here to inspire you in everything you wish for and pursue.

As a kindred spirit to her husband and partner, Santa, Mrs. Claus shares his generosity, joviality, and special talent for engaging with children. She is an adventurous and resilient heroine who has been featured in Christmas stories for nearly two centuries.

Mrs. Claus sees that Santa is well-prepared for his annual Christmas Eve journey, and oversees toy production at the North Pole. It is she who ensures Christmas arrives precisely on schedule.

As an empowered character, she contributes to the Christmas festivities in her own right, including organizing and attending too many charitable events to mention.

The enchanting Mrs. Claus represents the resounding potential in all of us.

This kind-hearted and nurturing soul is renowned for her exceptional cookies and the festive meals she prepares in her warm, cozy kitchen. Mrs. Claus is cherished by all who know her for her calm, loving ways. Her steadfast commitment to carrying kindness and joy associated with Christmas beyond December creates a lasting impact on all whom she encounters.

Mrs. Claus understands what it takes to keep all the baubles in the air with so much to do as Christmas approaches. She invites you to Christmas at the Clauses' and offers suggestions for decorating and entertaining, as well as how to avoid becoming stressed with the flurry of activities that come with the holidays.

"I never in my life could do so much for boys and girls without so good a wife!"

- Santa Claus (1886)

CHAPTER 1

The Essence of Mrs. Claus

Hello, Mrs. Claus, how wonderful to be speaking to you today. I am so very pleased you agreed to answer some questions for our readers. Is it true that everyone at the North Pole, including Santa, comes to you when they need advice?"

I have lived a fabulous life and have gained the gift of wisdom along the way through my adventures and experiences. It is an honor to be asked to listen to others or to answer their questions. To be a good and *active* listener, take in everything being said, without judgment. If someone asks for my advice, I am happy to offer my thoughts and considerations. However, I often find it the most helpful to allow the person time and space to express their own ideas. I can then offer to help them find options by asking questions that clarify or expand the discussion. Offering someone time to listen to their story, a problem, or a challenge is a very kind thing to do. My advice is to be generous with your time and to become the best listener you can be.

What are your talents, Mrs. Claus, aside from being the world's best cookie baker?

I am highly confident, and this has allowed me to try a great many experiences - from taking our magical sleigh on solo rides, to snowboarding, and piloting a plane. I do not view confidence as someone's belief that they are particularly skilled or good at something, but rather as the belief in your own ability to find a way to accomplish something. "I will succeed, even if it means I try, and try again," as I often say. It is a mindset of adaptability and of what I refer to as falling forward. In trying and possibly failing, you learn and gather skills. When you fail and fall forward, you dust yourself off, get back up, and carry on. Falling forward time and time again requires high confidence. This powerful mindset is needed to persevere and to eventually succeed. I often remind the Elves at the North Pole that "Where There is a Wish, There is a Way."

Many readers will be familiar with who you are, but is there anything specific that you would like to share with them?

I'm both the CEO - Christmas Executive Officer - and the Postmaster General here at the North Pole. I oversee all the incoming letters at our post office. I sometimes look at the huge stack of mail and wonder how the Elves and I will get it all sorted, with each letter read, and with the children's requests added to the lists. Then I remember one of our Claus family mottoes, which is, "the more, the merrier." Those four simple words pull me through.

I read all the new Christmas books published each year. I have an extensive library, and I write book reviews, so books with special merit get the attention they deserve. I am happy to support authors in this way. Perhaps your readers would like to send me a book recommendation? I would be pleased to hear from them.

My days are also spent helping the reindeer and Elves appreciate their own brilliance. At the North Pole, we celebrate and appreciate one another every day. It is a big part of why the North Pole is the happiest place imaginable.

I find it interesting that some stories portray me as rather grumpy, resentful, and dull. Some also suggest that I do not have my own adventures, which couldn't be further from the truth! I have a very sunny disposition with rarely a cloudy day, I don't allow resentment to get to me, and I am anything but dull.

I have taken over the reins and delivered the toys to boys and girls on many occasions when Santa was sick or injured and could not make his way.

The first time I flew the sleigh by myself, I was nervous. It was Christmas Eve, and Santa had broken his leg, so he couldn't get in and out of the chimneys and houses to make the deliveries quickly enough. I was frightened to make the trip on my own, but the reindeer knew the flight path so well that I was sure we would get everywhere we needed to go. Before I took off into the cold, clear night sky, I took a few deep breaths and reminded myself to be brave and to find my confidence because the children were counting on me, and we Clauses always deliver! The reindeer and I made our way, and after the last gift was safely under the tree of the last house, I arrived back home safe and sound. I have successfully saved Christmas on multiple occasions, I am proud to say!

I will tell you of one of my favorite adventures. As with many adventures, I didn't set out to be on one. Once upon a time, I was just walking in the winter forest when I noticed a baby reindeer all by itself. So, I approached the reindeer, and I asked it if it wanted help. The reindeer nodded and said, "Please." I introduced myself, and she told me her name was Harmony. I knew those woods so well that I was able to find and follow reindeer tracks to bring her back to her herd. Not long after she was safely home, I heard sleigh bells coming over the hill. A sleigh stopped in front of me, and out jumped Santa Claus himself! He was delighted that I found the little lost reindeer, who belonged to one of his many nomadic herds. He thanked me for coming to the doe's rescue, and asked if I would consider joining him to help with the reindeer at the North Pole. That is how I met Santa and came to live here. My forest adventure was the first day of our enduring love story.

I had always known that I wanted to be involved in making the world a better place for children and animals, but I did not know where that journey would begin or take me. I was not sure how I was going to achieve it, but I knew in my heart that this was what I wanted. There I was standing amongst the reindeer, meeting Santa. It was the most perfect of opportunities with luck sprinkled in. I heard the reindeer calling out for help, I heard the sleigh bells that came over the hill, and I knew my dream was about to come true.

What is your first name, Mrs. Claus?

There have been hundreds of stories, poems, songs, plays, and film scripts written that include me, and they gave me names like Carol, Holly, Gertrude, Bessie, Layla, Jessie, Anya, Mary, and Joan. Santa is the only one who knows and calls me by my first name, but I love it when children call me by my magical names - Mrs. Claus or Mother Christmas - best of all.

Mrs. Claus, would you please describe for the readers how you like to dress?

I express my creativity by dressing in a way that is colorful, playful, and merry, in Christmas colors and fun patterns. Today, I'm wearing peppermint stripes and snowflakes. I love a sparkly piece of snowflake jewelry. I have poinsettia flowers tucked behind my ear, because they feel fun and festive - a little extra pop of color in my silver hair. I accessorize in fun ways, and I love wearing perfumes that make me happy. Right now, my perfume is a combination of peppermint and sugar cookie scents.

It is surprising for some people that I sometimes wear pants. I spend a lot of time in the stables with the reindeer. I'm certainly not going to wear one of my long, pretty dresses to go play with animals! I remember a time in the past when women were not permitted to wear pants in public, nor were women permitted to vote in elections or to work in certain jobs. Fortunately, we changed all of that, although it took a great many voices, including mine, to bring real change for women. At the North Pole, Santa and I are equal partners, with equality of effort as an important cornerstone of our marriage. We share a dream, and we work together to make it come true.

Are people surprised by your appearance?

Always! I've frequently experienced the phenomenon of walking into a room and being aware that there is looking, pointing, and whispering. I'm aware that my appearance is having an impact, but if I sense it is less than positive, I don't allow it to affect my self-confidence. Children appreciate the way I dress and the special attention I give, and they especially enjoy peeking inside my Peppermint Purse. It is full of things that they will delight in holding or seeing.

Some people have expectations that Mrs. Claus only wears glasses on the end of her nose, an apron tied around her waist, and a little mop cap holding her hair back. I love to bake for others, but this one look need not define me. I am so much *more* than that. It doesn't require bravery to present yourself in a creative way when you're living as your authentic self. Getting *to* our authentic self and being comfortable with our decision to chart our own fashion path can require a measure of courage. I dress to delight the children I meet, while also keeping myself comfortable and happy.

How do you handle quizzical remarks about your style of dress?

My response is typically, "I know this look might not be for everyone, but it's giving me joy and happiness today." I acknowledge that it's not for you, but it *is* for me. There's nothing wrong with people not seeing eye-to-eye, but it is surprising how many people choose to share anything other than a compliment or kind word about the way someone else chooses to dress. When I was young, I learned from the fairies that it is far greater to honor the person themselves, rather than the outfit they have on.

When people get to know me, and they realize that the way I dress is just me, they become excited and gracious. "Where did you get your shoes?" is a common question I am asked, and I am quick to reply that they are made for me by our incredible shoemaker Elves. I make my own dresses and hats, as well as my capes and coats.

Are there other ways you share your creativity?

Dressing in a creative fashion is just one of the ways I express my artistic nature and authentic self. Other creative pursuits I enjoy include writing, scrapbooking, drawing, baking, canning and making jam, singing, storytelling, knitting, embroidery, crocheting, pottery, making storyboards, and gardening. I love learning languages, and am fluent in Elvish, which makes storytelling with the Elves so much fun! I enjoy exploring the magical world I live in and often spend time collecting Northern Lights dust to discover new ways we can use it, beyond helping the reindeer take flight.

One of my favorite creative activities is decorating and entertaining for the holidays. At the North Pole, we celebrate not just Christmas, but many holidays. I am always excited to bring out our collection of cherished decorations and place them around our home. Our Christmas decorations include everything from rare ornaments to whimsical items that Santa and I have collected, been given, or that I have made. Perhaps my favorite items are the festively dressed teddy bears and the baskets of storybooks that we place under the tree each year. Young Elves enjoy picking a story to be read aloud or to take home from these baskets. I am also very fond of my star collection, which I keep on display throughout the year.

"The world truly is so full of so many wonderful things that we can all be so very happy."

- Mrs. Claus

Mrs. Claus, do you know how much your efforts are appreciated?

That is kind of you to ask, but Santa and I do not look for recognition or even gratitude for our efforts. All the gratitude we desire comes from knowing that children experience exceptional joy at Christmas. Santa and I practice anonymous giving. Sending a gift or money anonymously to someone reflects selflessness, grounded in compassion and love.

If you know that someone has gone out of their way to give you something or has done something for you, it is always nice to thank them. My advice is to let them know that their generosity touched you in a special and meaningful way. When I receive a gift, I thank the person and explicitly state what it is I am thanking them for. If someone does something kind, mention the deed or act in the thank you. "Thank you for taking my dog for a walk today. I really appreciate this act of kindness." "Thank you for your cheery words. I needed a smile today!" Write and mail, or leave behind, thank you cards, and encourage children to do the same. Send a child a special card, or thank you note, and you might just hear them say with a grin, "Well, well, well – what do we have here?"

CHAPTER 2

Year-Round Happiness and Joy

How do you achieve year-round happiness and joy, Mrs. Claus?

Thank you for asking such an important question. I view happiness as a constant part of my life, rather than as a temporary, fleeting moment. I remind myself regularly of the reasons I do what I do. I ask myself if my activities are creating more joy for myself and others, or if they are holding me or others back. I remain open to making changes. It takes commitment to live like this, but the results are so spectacular that I cannot imagine living in any other way.

Engaging in storytelling, reading books, or reciting poetry, or singing with children or the elderly brings me great joy. I prepare well ahead for my visits outside of the North Pole to ensure that the activity I have planned for an engagement will be well-received. I enjoy listening to personal Christmas stories and childhood memories from those whom I meet. I like to start my storytelling with something that excites the audience and gets their attention: I might start by asking, "Do you know the difference between a Snow Fairy and a Frost Fairy?" I then follow with questions to get creative minds thinking: "Do you know that Snow Fairies design every snowflake that falls on your nose, tongue, and eyelashes, and that it is the Frost Fairies who decorate your windows with beautiful frost patterns and create winter wonderlands?"

"Do you know that Snow and Frost Fairies stay away from hot stoves in warm, friendly kitchens? You will never find a North Pole Fairy roasting their toes by a blazing winter fire, or wearing sweaters or wool socks to stay cozy." "Snow Fairies and Frost Fairies positively love ice cream, as does our dearest Santa Claus. What flavor do you think Santa likes best of all?"

I pride myself on my penmanship, and it is a pleasure to copy a favorite poem or recipe when requested to do so. I enjoy making greeting cards. Sending Christmas cards is a wonderful way to stay connected with friends and family. Personalizing cards with remarks, or including a letter, a poem, a photo, or a recipe, makes them even more special. One of the key sources of my abounding happiness is staying connected to my friends.

Whether walking through the woods, stargazing in the wee hours, observing the Aurora Borealis, or caring for our reindeer, I am the happiest when I am in the natural world. The Earth is full of beauty and magic at every turn. There is a peace that comes from connecting with animals, especially our beloved pets. Their loyalty is a remarkable gift they give to us. The wide expanse of the sky, the feel of the earth under my feet, and the music of the outdoors are comforts in the bustle of everyday life that I enjoy every day.

I have prepared some questions that may help prompt you to find your own sources of year-round happiness and joy. May one or more of these questions ignite a spark in an area of your life that needs a good polish to really shine!

What brings you contentment?
What brings you joy?
What brings you happiness?
Where is the light in your world?
Are you building strong connections?
Do you feel engaged with the world?
Have you recently answered a call to action?
Are you engaged in meaningful pursuits?
Did you celebrate a small success in the past day?
Did you applaud someone else's success in the past week?
Do you believe that positive change is possible?
What needs to change for happiness to flourish?
Do you believe an abundance of joy is available to you?

Journaling brings me a sense of fulfilment and contentment. Looking back over the pages of my life, I reconnect with what has gone before and remember individuals who have added a spark to my own life. I enjoy reflective time when I am alone, and can quietly read my beloved books, revisiting my scrapbooks, or looking through my treasure chest of mementos. I keep an ongoing list of everything I love and appreciate. I encourage you to start by simply writing the words "I love," and noting what comes up for you. It is fun to do this with children, and to hear or read their responses!

I love milk chocolate. Eating milk chocolate invokes happy memories of my childhood and of celebrations. I love the home I share with Santa. Every item in our home is something both Santa and I truly enjoy. If you live with others, ask them before you recycle any household item or make major changes that may impact them. Involve children in changes to their personal spaces or the removal of their personal possessions. Next, try this with the meals you prepare and work to develop love lists in all areas of your life.

In concluding on your question on how your readers can increase their own capacity for joy and happiness, I offer the following suggestion: reflect on times in your life when charity, generosity, kindness, and thoughtfulness contributed to your own sense of joy and happiness. Recall a time when you used the Golden Rule, treating others in the way you like to be treated, or used your power of selflessness, putting the needs of others ahead of your own.

May this inspire you to repeat what has been successful in the past. When your life is based on delivering on these principles, you will find joy and happiness even in times of trial.

"By treating others as you like to be treated, you contribute to creating a more compassionate world."

– Mrs. Claus

CHAPTER 3

You May Be A Mrs. Claus When You...

Approach a challenge with positive expectations
Perform a request without expecting praise or reciprocation
Do what needs to be done, despite not feeling enthusiastic about doing it
Consider the impact your actions may have on others
Catch snowflakes on your tongue and eyelashes
Infuse your hairbrush with peppermint essential oils
Wear a red party dress
Wish upon a star
Shop with a list, check it twice, and buy only what is needed
Put a personal pursuit on hold to attend an important family event
Decorate with fairy lights
Recite "'Twas the Night Before Christmas" to a toddler
Teach a child about Mother Goose and her nursery rhymes

Carve a pumpkin
Celebrate Winter Solstice
Make a wish when blowing out candles on your birthday cake
Help someone's wish come true
Remind a friend of their gifts and capabilities
Place a donation in a charity box
Organize a children's Easter egg hunt
Give someone your undivided attention for more than a few minutes
Celebrate a friend's success
Decorate a Christmas tree
Remember to breathe when you're frightened
Celebrate Christmas in July
Smile back at yourself in the mirror after applying lipstick
Dress in clothing to delight a child
Keep a promise to yourself
Make an appointment and keep it
Say "good morning" to a stranger
Host a cookie exchange party
Gift a favorite book from your childhood to a child
Sing a song from your early years to help you fall asleep
Spark love by playing the "matchmaker"

Mrs. Claus, I've heard you say that you live with the spirit of Christmas in your heart. How can someone achieve this state of mind?

Living with Christmas in your heart is a way of living happily ever after. This way of thinking views each new day as an opportunity for joy. I use a few short phrases to remind myself of what it is that I hold fast to. Choose your own phrases, and keep them to a few words, so that they will be easy to remember. Make sure you believe in their message wholeheartedly. Or adopt the following sayings into your own life, and may they serve you well, as they have me.

Life is a Gift

Each new day is full of potential for happiness. Appreciate how far you've come. Your past created who you are today, but today, your past rests softly in your heart and memories. Today is a new day that comes with a chance to share and foster love, and to give and receive kindness and joy. Find and embrace the light in your world. Today is a day to be happy.

Make Your Life Come True

Be the hero or heroine of your own story! You are the main character who meets the moment, the author of your adventures. Tell your story in your own voice. Whether it is your next chapter, next paragraph, or next sentence, you'll never be stuck with a blank page, for your story and life develop with each new day.

Are you the hero or heroine in your own story? If not, ask why it isn't you? Santa is the main character of his story, and I'm the main character of mine. I have the agency to make my life come true, and that includes asking for help when I need it.

Christmas is a Feeling

It is far more than just one day on the calendar. Acts of kindness and thoughtfulness affect how happy you and others feel. Choose to act with a giving heart, fostering a spirit of generosity every day, and finding opportunities to uplift others.

"When people experience kindness, they are more likely to pass it on."

– Mrs. Claus

"If it rains on your parade, put up your umbrella and carry on."

– Mrs. Claus

Dear Reader,

I would like you to know that I am the keeper of wishes. You might not know that I am the one who listens for wishes cast upon the stars. Trust that your wishes are heard. Wishes can come true when you believe in endless possibilities. You are never too old to look up and wish upon a star! Your wish is your heart's desire. Casting a wish involves a dose of good luck, a measure of faith, an abundance of trust, and an unwavering belief that the future is bright and that dreams and wishes can come true. Say your wish aloud, share it with the universe, or share it with me. Believe in yourself above all else. It is never too late to start over, nor to make the changes necessary to make real progress.

"You are never too old to be proud of yourself for making changes that improve your life. Say out loud, 'I did it. I wished for this, and now it is happening.'"

- Mrs. Claus

Wishes that come to my attention are written upon ribbons, hung on a special magical tree that grows in the polar forest. Only those wishes that Santa cannot deliver by sleigh are hung on the tree. All who pass by the tree read a wish, and contribute, if they can, to making it come true. Sometimes, I take the reindeer and sleigh and travel far, whispering the wish into the ear of someone who is well-suited to help. Santa sometimes finds a wish tucked under a tree in a child's home and brings it back on his return from delivering presents. We read and work on those wishes in the New Year. In making wishes, be open to receiving them in ways you might not expect. For instance, when a loved one has passed on, whether they are a family member, a friend, or a pet, Santa and I often hear a wish that they can return. Our magic works differently…we cannot bring them back, but you can tell us stories about them, and bring them up to your heart, and to ours. In that way, your loved ones are always with you, and with anyone who hears their stories.

Merry always, Mrs. Claus

CHAPTER 4

Mrs. Claus' "Fa-La-La" Philosophy

Mrs. Claus, are there any specific tips you can offer the readers for making wishes?

The act of wishing reflects your inner optimism. Frame wishes with a positive attitude. Wish with determination and clarity for the best results and use their motivational force to fuel actions. Wishes are dreams with a plan of action. Find the balance between commitment and remaining open to adapting incrementally, if necessary. Celebrate small victories and visualize your wish coming true. Practice patience. Seize the opportunity to make wishes, wish upon a star, make a wish while blowing out birthday candles, or when you find a penny on the path.

Mrs. Claus, what is your "Fa-La-La" Philosophy?

My "Fa-La-La" Philosophy is based on trusted truisms that I will share with you. "Fa-La-La" means finding the merry in all you say and do. Laughter is best, and I remind myself to laugh often as children do. While Santa is known for his "ho ho ho," he's not the only one who laughs and giggles that way! We are both incredibly jolly people, and that giggle is a Claus family trait. Smiles and laughter are wonderfully contagious. A playful, merry twinkle travels all the way from your face down to your toes. Try it - start with a smile and see where it goes! Santa and I understand the power of a smile. A smile is so often reflected. Try smiling, and witness how the others spontaneously smile back at you. We both have Christmas jokes ready in case someone needs a laugh or a giggle. Have you a joke to tell? Do you have a funny Christmas sweater? When was the last time you cried with laughter?

"There will always be stormy days, but remember, you choose your responses and the actions you take."

- Mrs. Claus

What did the salt say to
the pepper at Christmas?

How much does Santa
pay to park his sleigh?

What makes the Elf Alphabet
different from everyone else's?

Where do Elves keep
their money?

Answers to the jokes on the previous page:

Season's Greetings

Nothing, it's on the house!

Noel

In a snowbank

As children, we spend much time playing and being creative with our friends. As we get older, we can forget the value of playing as we get bogged down in serious pursuits. There is always a snowball in my Peppermint Purse! At the North Pole, we love a good snowball fight. Bring out the board games, the costume box, or the ring toss. Make a date with your friends for a potluck, wreath-making party, or a Secret Santa gift exchange. At the North Pole, we host a "'Twas the Night Before Christmas" Pajama Party a week before the big night itself. I read the wonderful poem, "'Twas the Night Before Christmas" aloud. Everyone dresses in Christmas pajamas. It is one of the most playful and jolly events of the year. I serve pancakes in fun shapes, with fruit toppings and whipped cream piled high. The young Elves are invited to decorate gingerbread houses, they bob for apples. I play the piano as they gather round to sing Christmas carols and songs.

When was the last time you attended a party in a playful costume?

Did you dress up in costume on Halloween or on Christmas in July?

The "Fa-La-La" Philosophy and Relationships

Each evening ends with Santa and I telling each other about the highlight of our day. It can be as simple as how much we enjoyed a warm chocolate chip cookie or the pleasure of a walk in the forest. This single question invokes a sense of appreciation for the day, and always puts a smile on my face, as it does Santa's, and is a "Fa-La-La" ending to the busy day.

Santa and I most certainly never go to bed annoyed with one another, and if we have something that we need to discuss, we do it and resolve it, well before our heads hit our pillows.

The past is the past, what is done cannot be undone, and tomorrow is another new day to try a little (or a lot) harder. We find that sorting out problems before they grow in proportion is the best strategy for a happy marriage. Problems, like runaway snowballs, need to be stopped in their tracks. If allowed to roll downhill, they have the tendency to take on momentum and grow exponentially.

It may surprise some readers to learn that Santa and I do not keep a Naughty List, as we do not harbor ill thoughts of past acts. When children tell us that they are worried that they may not be on the Nice List, we tell them that "it is called the '*Nice* List,' not the '*Perfect* List.' All that we ask is that you try to do your best."

We make it our practice to encourage, rather than to criticize. We would never speak in a way that would undermine a child's self-confidence. We refrain from asking a child if they have been well-behaved or good, for in this question is a seed of doubt. Instead, we ask them to tell us about their friends, or what they have recently enjoyed doing, or perhaps what they have planned for the rest of the day. We take an interest in them, and we do so with our full attention. We then praise and applaud their accomplishments. Our belief in them is unwavering, and we let them know it in our response.

We replace the word "no" with the word "please." Children hear the word "no" a lot, as we use the word "no" to keep them safe, but there are other ways to engage with children. You'll hear me say, "Please walk, I want you to stay safe," instead of, "No, don't run." "Please" is a request, not a command. When you start with "please," that is a magical word, and it demonstrates respect. Santa and I often only have a few moments with children, and we make sure to make a lasting impact that resonates in kindness, respect, and love.

You will remember the story of the poor little reindeer and how his playmates would not allow him to play in their reindeer games. With his special nose, he went on to become Santa's star on one stormy Christmas Eve. Santa did not add the other reindeer to a Naughty List, but gave them that special look he can give, which inspired them to change their ways. Santa has a special talent for reminding people of their inherent goodness and kindness. It is one of his most admirable qualities.

One for All, and All for One

Instead of being one up against the world, adopting the attitude of being "one for all, and all for one" can be transformative. Christmas couldn't happen the way that it does each year without us, the Clauses, Elves, and reindeer, working together as a team to spread magic and joy. We work towards one common goal, and that teamwork gives us drive, purpose, and connection. Imagine what that could look like and feel like in your own life, every day. How can you be a teammate to others? What acts of selflessness can you contribute to making the world a gentler place? This is how a "Fa-La-La" way of life is so incredibly magical.

The More, The Merrier

"The More the Merrier" means pulling up an extra chair, setting another place, or hanging one more stocking. "The More, the Merrier" involves being aware of the needs of others, extending hospitality, and making sure no one feels left out. It is a delightful way to be in the world, with a smile and an invitation at the ready. Santa and I open our home one night a week to all who want to join us for supper. I make a delicious soup, and put out a variety of breads with a selection of toppings. Everyone is welcome to visit. After we have supped, we sing songs with all voices joining in, and our guests take turns reading poetry and stories aloud. It is a time to build friendships and to appreciate one another in our North Pole community.

"The more participants in any activity, the more enjoyable it will be."

- Mrs. Claus

As CEO of the North Pole, how do you interact with grumpy Elves?

Let me share a little story with you. I was checking in with the Elves in the toymaking workshop, and one of the Elves was having a tough day. I greeted her warmly, and she furrowed her brow, made the tiniest little sound, and didn't look up. She seemed troubled. This wasn't like her at all! Usually, she greets me back, smiles brightly, and strikes up a conversation.

"Would you like to tell me about your day?" I asked, gently. She shook her head and kept her eyes low. "Of course. I understand. I am here any time you'd like to talk about it, and I'll see you tomorrow." I moved on to say hello to the next Elf.

When encountering frustration or grumpiness, I find it surprising when people take a reaction like this grumpy one as a personal insult. A good place to start is accepting that it is not personal, but rather someone, in this case, a Toymaking Elf, having a tough moment. My advice in situations such as these is to show you care and then to give them their space. It is simply counter-productive and rather silly to meet grumpiness with negativity. Making the situation easier, never harder, is my policy in tricky situations.

You will be happy to know that, after a little time had passed, so had her grumpiness and her troubles, and she came to tell me all about it. A little distance and time are often the best remedy.

How do you handle complaints, Mrs. Claus?

If you hear a criticism of your own actions, find the right time to come together with the person involved. Be specific about what you would like to accomplish when you engage to resolve the issue. This will help the listener receive what you have to say.

Acknowledge the other person's point of view before elaborating on your own. You might say, "I understand your viewpoint on this matter. I would like to explore other ideas that might work for both of us." Ask yourself before you speak, "Why am I saying this now? What do I hope to accomplish?" Be honest with yourself, and you will find it is much easier to stay honest with others in the way you communicate.

Santa and I are open with one another. We share a deep level of trust. Allowing your partner to express themselves, without hesitation or pretense, forms the most wonderful and intimate connection. Santa sees me, hears me, and knows me because I showed up in our relationship as my true, authentic self. If you do not share who you really are with those close to you, then you risk being confused with someone else. Being seen and heard is tremendously important to overall happiness.

Santa and I live a magical life. Our happily ever after is helping others with their wishes and dreams. It is wonderful that we share the same life purpose, and we celebrate each other's accomplishments. Open and honest communication, deep and abiding trust, and love are all bedrocks of our very successful marriage and partnership. At the North Pole, while we each have our own responsibilities, it is the planned, intentional time and shared experiences that keep us close as partners. Santa is my best friend, and I am his. I would not say anything about Santa to someone else that I would not say to him directly, and that fosters the intimacy that binds us.

CHAPTER 5

Christmas Is Coming

I find myself overwhelmed during the lead-up to Christmas. Do you have any advice for me, Mrs. Claus?

Take the time to remind yourself of the things that put you in the spirit of Christmas. Perhaps it is the music, baking, decorations, or classic stories and movies. Perhaps it is making that special Christmas outfit for a darling grandchild, or preparing the guest room with special festive touches for the visitors soon to arrive. Perhaps it is getting tickets to a Christmas live show, or creating an evergreen garland for the staircase, or putting out pictures taken at Christmas over the years.

Without fail, I write up a Christmas plan to make sure that all the things that are important to me are not missed. I love making lists and checking them twice, so when I am heading into the busy Christmas season, I write lists to prioritize the things that need to be done and that I care about. It is from this perspective that I build my plan. It is not a cookie-cutter plan written by someone else, but one of my own creations. I use this well-crafted plan to prevent myself from becoming overwhelmed.

Writing Christmas cards is important to me, for it builds connections that can last a lifetime. Connecting with my friends and family far away brings me great pleasure, so Christmas cards go on the list. Making traditional foods also goes on the list. I need to prepare all the ingredients well ahead of time for the preserves, Christmas pudding, sugar cookies, and shortbread that everyone enjoys so much. I will schedule time to try out new recipes that have come my way. Variety is the spice of life, I have heard it said – and I agree! I love tradition, and rituals offer comfort and stability, but trying something new is fun and exciting.

I must add an entertaining tip here, which is that I only serve to my guests that which I have *previously* made and discovered to be extraordinary. This tip will help you avoid the stress that comes from experimenting on the day and finding yourself serving your guests items that are less than super-delicious.

Next, I plan out the time needed for all the decorations, including those for the tree. I love putting our heirloom decorations and my personal star collection on the lovely branches. I also enjoy trees set about the house with creative themes. I consider all that will be needed to make the parties that will be held here at the North Pole a great success. After I have made my notes and lists, I assign each of the tasks to a special calendar. I keep a separate list of things that I may find the time to do but are not essential. Setting time limits and delivery dates is a way to eliminate the seasonal pressure and the feeling of being overwhelmed.

I review the plan and decide who I can call upon to assist. Christmas is very much a group affair, and tasks are to be shared. Work the plan, and do not let the plan work you. Remember, as in all things in life, to stay open and flexible. Christmas comes around every year. If your merry self is to be maintained throughout the season, there is always *next* year to do what may end up needing to be skipped this year.

Are you always cheerful, Mrs. Claus, even as you count down to Christmas with all the things that you must do?

Like everyone, I have my moments. It is essential to take care of yourself and to recognize when you need to take a step back and rebalance or rest. When I am feeling out of sync, I have found that it helps to review how I am spending my time. I ask myself if there is an area of my life that needs attention. Being mindful of where you are using your energy, can bring you back to a place of balance, calm, and good cheer.

I take time each morning to check in with myself, reviewing my lists and my calendar, and to notice how I am feeling – perhaps even naming what comes up for me with a word, or a color. I check my emotions as I would check the weather. If my feelings might be cloudy and a chance of rain, it is a sign that today, I may need to take special care to read, write, draw, or spend time outside in the fresh air with the reindeer, or take my snowshoes and head out on an adventure.

After this, I review what needs to be done today, the promises made that need to be kept, and the tasks, big and small. I make sure to have time with Santa and share fun and laughter with the Elves. I also check in with my physical being. Does my body need a walk, or a stretch, or a nap today? I also check my breathing to see if it is even and deep. I learned from the reindeer that alternate-nostril breathing is a fast way to improve my overall well-being.

Reindeer Alternate Nostril Breathing. Close off one nostril with your finger and then breathe in and out through the open nostril. Reverse and repeat ten times until you are breathing evenly on both sides. Even nostril breathing is very important to your overall health and well-being. The reindeer practice this daily, as do I.

Hot Chocolate Breathing. I imagine I've got a mug of hot chocolate in front of me, and I breathe in, rounding out my belly. Slowly blow on the hot chocolate to help it cool. Repeat several times, until you feel your heart rate and your thoughts slow. Imagine the warmth of the hot cocoa, and focus on your breathing. The wonderful thing about using this to de-stress is that it is always with you and just takes a moment to remember to find your breath.

Another tip is to put your hands over your head, opening your rib cage, and making breathing easier. You can imagine having big, beautiful, glistening angel or fairy wings while you are doing this.

It is easy to become overwhelmed with many demands placed on your time and energy. I value these little rituals and hope you will come to use them as well. Perhaps you already do!

When I find myself with so many things to do that I do not know where to start, I perform what I call my "power hour." I'll write a list of ten small things that I can do in one hour when I find myself being less productive or spinning around in circles (which does happen from time to time for me, as it does for everyone else). This list of ten small things sets me on a path of action. When the hour is up, I honor my accomplishment by saying, "I did everything on the list!" out loud.

What do you do when you are out of sorts or underwhelmed, Mrs. Claus?

I love learning and find it very uplifting. Poke your nose into a book or article on something you know nothing about and prepare to find yourself refreshed and remarkably uplifted. If I ever have a cloudy day, I set out to learn something new and to share what I have learned with someone else. It works wonders, and I hope you try this for yourself. Many times, Santa has heard me proclaim in an excited tone, "I did not know that – I am amazed!"

If I am feeling out of sorts, I will put my feet up with a cup of tea and a treat such as warm fruit toast spread with flavored butter. Fairy butter is an heirloom recipe from my godmother - the Queen of the Fairies. The other heirloom recipes that are shared here were given to me by Santa's own grandmother – Mother Goose herself.

Fairy Butter

You Will Need

2 eggs

1 tablespoon orange or rose water

2 teaspoons sugar

4 ounces of butter slightly softened

Edible flowers or herbs or colored sugar to garnish

Instructions

Boil the eggs. Cool completely in ice water.

Peel and separate the egg yolks from the egg whites.

Using a mortar and pestle, mash the egg yolks, add flower water, and sugar forming a fine paste.

Add the butter and mix well. Using a strainer and a large spoon push the mixture through the holes, making strands.

Garnish and serve with warm sweet breads.

These butters make a welcome gift presented in a pretty jar or dish.

Cinnamon Orange Honey Butter

You Will Need

½ cup of softened butter

¼ cup honey

2 teaspoons orange zest

½ teaspoon of ground cinnamon

Instructions

Combine the ingredients well. Serve with fruit breads, toast or crackers.

Cranberry Honey Butter

You Will Need

1 cup butter, softened

⅓ cup minced dried cranberries

¼ cup of honey

2 teaspoons orange zest

pinch of salt

Instructions
Combine all the ingredients well, serve. Refrigerate any leftover.

CHAPTER 6

I Believe In You

"While you may not have always believed in me, I believe in you."

- Mrs. Claus

Some people encounter feelings of sadness during the holidays. What words of comfort would you offer them, Mrs. Claus?

These situations call for your special attention and care. Begin with empathy, recognizing and honoring the person's feelings and views. Then, if appropriate, extend to them an invitation to join you in a future activity. This is important, as it offers them something to look forward to. The invitation can, but does not need to, involve a Christmas activity. This gesture demonstrates to the person that you're thinking of them. Anticipating a pleasant future activity is both motivational and uplifting. One of the greatest thrills in childhood is the anticipation of Santa's arrival. You may remember waiting for Christmas as being more than half the fun!

If you are feeling melancholy or saddened due to missing someone who is special to you during the holidays, put pleasurable activities into your own calendar and commit to doing them. Plan out the details of the event, such as what you will wear, or how you will thank a host or hostess. Remind yourself that feelings are influenced by actions, and that feelings fade with time unless re-stimulated. Take care of the stories you repeat and the thoughts you are dwelling upon. Acknowledge uncomfortable feelings, while shifting your focus to actions that are positive. Take a walk in the fresh air, and put out photographs or items that bring you happiness, while putting away items that bring up harder emotions. Remember, your thoughts and feelings are like clouds in the sky - observe them, honor them, and know that they do not stay forever.

Treat yourself as you would a dear friend, with compassion and patience. Find solutions to problems where possible, ask for help when you need it, and set a date to resolve the issue. Know and accept that the actions you choose to take can improve how you feel.

Revisiting happy memories of Christmases past brings many people comfort and joy, but for others, looking back to the past brings feelings of discomfort and sadness. I have found it helpful to encourage individuals feeling this way to build new positive memories intentionally that can be recalled at a future date. Gaining the ability to access pleasant memories contributes to our overall sense of contentment with life in a meaningful way.

Consider what is needed to make an upcoming event memorable. In your planning, fill the experience with the senses, including delicious foods to taste, beautiful flowers to behold, or other visual elements, and wonderful smells and sounds. Take pictures or journal notes about the event. Building a memory takes some ingenuity and commitment, including proclaiming out loud – "Let's Make This Memorable." It takes a willingness and a conscious effort, but it is always worthwhile.

"Believe that today can be the making of tomorrow's happy memory."

\- Mrs. Claus

Write upcoming events in your calendar

Mark on your calendar the birthdays of your friends and colleagues and plan to send out birthday cards.

Celebrate the birthday of a favorite artist or person who has inspired you in a remarkable way.

Mark interesting events or milestones with celebrations.

Celebrate the many holidays throughout the year

We are a small group this year, and we have decided to not do the usual big Christmas. How can we make a smaller Christmas enjoyable?

There is something special about a calm or small Christmas with walks in the snow, thoughtful gifts, and time shared with loved ones. Calm Christmas is at the very heart of many Nordic cultures that embrace the concept of "hygge." Hygge (pronounced ˈhoogə or HUE-guh) embodies a sense of coziness, contentment, and well-being that is at the essence of life at the North Pole. It is the way we live every day.

Creating a hygge North Pole Christmas involves wrapping up in blankets, watching marshmallows melt in a steaming cup of hot cocoa, playing pin-the-tail on the reindeer, and reading Christmas poetry aloud to one another. It means taking a spontaneous break at the North Pole Toy Workshop to enjoy a few laughs and a sing-along. It is a Christmas tree, decorated with strings of handmade ornaments, dried oranges, and a popcorn and cranberry garland. It means making cut-out foil doily angels or paper bag stars. Hygge is a neighbor dropping by and being welcomed, without reservation. Hygge is decorating gingerbread cookies with the Elf children while candles flicker on the mantle. Christmas is a feeling, and it can be found in the grand as it can in the smallest hygge corner.

Mrs. Claus, did you and Santa have help in making your dream to provide for children as you do come true?

I had help along the way in making my dream come true. My godmother is the Queen of the Fairies, and she bestowed a gift of a magical purse of gold on me on my marriage to Santa. Her gift provides for all that we need at the North Pole, including the materials for all the toys that we create and build. We are all supported by one another in miraculous fashion: for a moment, consider your connection to all the people involved in producing the book you hold in your hands.

From the people who planted the tree, to the ones who made the paper, to the bookbinders, printers, authors, and artists, to the friend who put the book into your hands, all these people had *you* in mind.

If you ever feel alone or not supported, think about the people *behind* the things that surround you, and remind yourself that the world is here for you at every turn. It's a beautiful thing to think about.

What can I do when my hard work isn't being recognized, including all the preparations and shopping I do for Christmas?

Resentment builds when you feel obliged to perform duties or tasks. For many people, Christmas is full of traditions and long-held practices that come with a high level of expectations regarding how they will be implemented. To avoid becoming resentful, do not agree to do things that do not align with your values. Avoid agreeing to requests that you think will place too high a burden on your time or resources. Feeling obliged to do something can be an uncomfortable feeling, stifle creativity, and build resentment. I have found that if I am being asked to do something that I am not comfortable with, it is best to find others to help or to share in the responsibility. I can then find the best way to participate without feeling resentful. I may also, on review of the request, politely decline.

Christmas time invites each of us to experience our own sense of wonderment. The twinkling lights, the melodious carols, and the festive decorations all contribute to an atmosphere of enchantment and wonder. Beyond these external manifestations, Christmas evokes a profound sense of connection and is filled with acts of sharing and caring. It is also a time to celebrate all that is merry and bright in the world. These are the ingredients that invoke a merry Christmas. Let not resentment spoil this for you – avoid it as best you can.

I have asked for help with the tree and the baking, but I am not getting the support I need. What shall I do, Mrs. Claus?"

As in any situation when you are working with a team or family members, the many aspects of Christmas need to be discussed, with each person's voice being heard and views respected. When your voice isn't being heard, ask again, or ask in a different way. Sometimes a written request can be more effective than a verbal request, or vice versa. Practice patience and prevail!

Chapter 7

A Time of Caring and Sharing

One of my favorite traditions is making holiday desserts. There is a centuries-old tradition in the British Isles of making Christmas pudding on "Stir-Up Sunday." Christmas puddings are dense, thick holiday dessert cakes, full of fruits and treacle (molasses) and on "Stir-Up Sunday" people over the years have gathered to assist in the stirring of the dense ingredients. Everyone who stirs gets to make a wish, and the group hides coins or charms in the pudding to give a little luck to the person who finds one of them in their pudding serving on Christmas. This is a tradition we continue each year at the North Pole. Time together, whether in the kitchen or around the table, is so special!

What traditions do you have in your own home around holiday meals or treats? Did you welcome a new family member or friend into your Christmas celebrations this past year and were they invited to share their own customs or family traditions at your holiday gatherings?

Are there desserts that you make every year that everyone looks forward to enjoying?

Chocolate Chip Gingerbread Cake

Makes one loaf

You Will Need

2 ½ cups flour

½ cup cocoa

1 teaspoon baking soda

1 ½ teaspoons ginger

1 teaspoon cinnamon

½ teaspoon salt

½ teaspoon allspice

¼ teaspoon cloves

¼ teaspoon nutmeg

¼ teaspoon black pepper

12 ounces miniature semisweet chocolate chips

2 tablespoons flour

¾ cup softened butter

1 ¼ cups sugar

1 teaspoon vanilla extract

2 large eggs

1 cup molasses

1 cup boiling water

Instructions:

Preheat oven to 350.

Grease a 10-cup Bundt pan with butter or non-stick spray, and dust with flour.

Toss chocolate chips with 2 tablespoons of flour and black pepper.

Beat softened butter with sugar and vanilla extract until light and fluffy.

At medium speed, beat eggs one at a time into butter and sugar.

Whisk together molasses and boiling hot water in a large glass bowl.

Mix flour with baking soda and spices.

At low speed, add the flour mixture in three equal parts to the butter, sugar mixture, alternating with ⅓ parts of the hot molasses mixture until the mixture is well blended.

Stir in the chocolate chips.

Pour batter into the pan and bake for 1 hour.

Cake is done when it starts to pull away from the pan. Serve with ice cream or sweetened whipped cream.

Cool on a baking rack and invert onto a plate after 20 minutes.

Dust with cocoa powder.

Mrs. Claus, would you please share your favorite books to read to children?

My top picks are the books that are especially wonderful when read aloud. Reading aloud "'Twas the Night Before Christmas" has been a cherished tradition by families for generations. This charming poem has been translated into every major language and is available in Braille. The poem was written by Clement Clarke Moore, who wrote the jolly piece as a present to his children on Christmas Eve of 1822! I enjoy reading the poem by pausing after each line and asking those gathered to call out the word that comes next: "'Twas The Night Before Christmas and all through the_____, Not a creature was stirring, not even a _____." Another playful way to engage an audience with the poem is to have them find the thirteen rhyme pairs that can be found. These rhyming pairs can also be placed on cards, and a game can be created based on the card games Memory or Go Fish.

Before/Store, Mouse/House, Sleep/Deep,

Dreams/Creams, Grace/Space, Door/Tore,

Stars/Bars, Aces/Faces, Love/Above,

True/Through, Joy/Boy, Good/Food, All/Stall

I highly recommend *Mrs. Willoughby's Christmas Tree* by Robert Barry and *Bear Stays Up For Christmas* by Karma Wilson as exceptional books to read aloud to young audiences. There are dozens of stories and poems that are creative interpretations of my own story that I think you will enjoy reading: A few of my favorites are "Goody Santa Claus" by Katherine Lee Bates and *Mrs. Claus Takes the Reins* by Sue Fliess. For adult audiences, I also highly recommend these stories: "The Gift of the Magi" by O. Henry, "Christmas Day in the Morning" by Pearl S. Buck, "The Greatest Gift" by Philip Van Doren Stern, and *Miracle on 34th Street* by Valentine Davies.

My child told me that they learned from a friend at school that there's no such thing as Santa Claus. What do I tell them?

Children have told me the very same thing. I reply by saying: "That had to have been a hard thing to hear. Let me ask you – what do *you* believe? Do you believe in kindness? Thoughtfulness? Hope? Wonder? Love? If you do, then you believe in all the things Santa and I *also* believe in and represent. This world always needs more people who can share all those wonderful things, and I believe that *you* are one of those people. While you may not believe in me, *I* believe in *you*."

Santa Claus and I are two of many characters who come to life in early childhood. Believing in us is one of a child's first experiences in embracing that which we can not see or hold, but that offers love and joy. Our lives are enriched by experiencing characters who share messages of love and demonstrate the finest of attributes through their stories. Santa Claus and our beloved characters from folktales, fairy tales, and modern stories are all instrumental in fostering the imagination and an appreciation for that which lies beyond the linear world, the place where dreams are created. I am part of that world.

"No one is ever too old to tuck a stuffie in their travel bag."

- Mrs. Claus

Do you ever feel like retiring or taking an extended break?

Hmm…I don't know that I've ever thought about that! Santa and I will take short vacations, but we're not retiring anytime soon. I've got several centuries left in me of this deeply meaningful work. Both Santa and I are grateful to wake up every morning so that we can continue to be the keepers of wishes and dreams. We will continue, I imagine, as long as people keep making them.

Mrs. Claus, how do you respond to a child who is timid upon meeting you or Santa Claus?

When I am in the company of children, I listen to and talk with them, never down to them. When they sit on my knee, a child is on the same level as I, and we engage as equals. I have seen many children who were shy and anxious when meeting Santa or me for the first time. Santa and I are always very careful to not rush a child, and it may take a moment to get them to cross the six-foot mark of separation. We like to think of that space as the "Goldilocks Zone" – not so close to we Clauses that they're uncomfortable, but not so far away that we can't see them and say hello. By recognizing and acknowledging that they may be a little frightened, we are thoughtful about making our voices gentler and taking care that we match their energy. We try to encourage them a little bit closer.

Sometimes, the child may be carrying a stuffed animal or a toy that you can ask them about. Other times, I go to my Peppermint Purse and bring out a toy of my own. I have a doll that I made many years ago, and she wears an outfit to match mine. I carry her to remind me that I can be brave, because when I have her with me, I am never alone. I step to the side, sit on the floor, and ask the nervous child if they would like to hold her, and borrow a bit of my bravery. Many times, they'll nod their head and sit on the floor beside me, holding my special doll.

How do we encourage thoughtfulness and kindness in the next generation?

Children learn the nature and value of thoughtfulness and kindness best when we "tall people" (because all of you are my beloved children in my eyes, and not adults) model it for them. In my experience, people genuinely like to help others and show this through acts of thoughtfulness and kindness. I believe people like to make other people happy. This can be something as small as opening a door for somebody whose hands are full, or stopping to assist someone who has dropped a package. Little acts of kindness show that someone else has noticed you. Remarking on the kindness of others to a child is one way to instill in them this enormously valuable human capability. It is an honor to be asked to help someone. Too often, we hesitate to ask for help.

When was the last time you were a hero or heroine? When was the last time you asked someone for their help in a difficult situation? Do you read children stories of brave heroes and heroines that model these qualities well?

Involving children directly in gift-giving or card exchanges is another way to instill a sense of thoughtfulness and kindness in children. Bring the child into the process of purchasing a present, wrapping it, and handing it to the recipient. Have children draw pictures on a card for special occasions, including birthdays. When the child attends a birthday party for one of their young friends, involve them in the choosing of the gift, instead of handing them a wrapped item to present.

Children can be offered an allowance at a young age with the promise that half of the money is for purchasing gifts for others for birthdays, Christmas, and other occasions, and the other half is for saving in their own piggy bank. This is a wonderful way to teach generosity and responsibility. If your first experiences with the exchange of money involve sharing, considering others, and generosity, the child is well on their way to developing a caring outlook that will flourish and bring them enormous satisfaction in life. We can also encourage children to make gifts, write a letter, write a story or a poem, or draw pictures as gifts, without the need for any monetary consideration. They might like to forage to find beautiful leaves or rocks in the forest, or a shell from a beach that they delight in and would love to give to someone.

Teach children the power of saying thank you. Everyone enjoys being recognized and valued. From small gestures that show we've been paying attention, to large demonstrations of gratitude, the thanks we give and receive make this world a warmer, merrier place. No matter how much we may need or want gratitude, it's not always easy to accept it, so open yourself up to receiving thanks. I know *I* love and appreciate you!

I love decorating cakes and cookies with children. They love being the ones in charge of putting the sprinkles on things, or the candles into a birthday cake before they're lit and ready to be blown out and wished upon. When they help with birthday candles, they're helping Santa and me with more wishes! Here is one of my favorite cookie recipes to make alongside children.

Mrs. Claus' Vanilla Sugar Cookies

Makes about 3 dozen small-to-medium sugar cookies

A cookie dough, straight from the North Pole, that doesn't need to chill before rolling it out and baking.

You Will Need

1 cup unsalted butter

1 cup granulated white sugar

1 teaspoon vanilla extract

1 egg

2 tsp baking powder

½ tsp salt

3 cups all-purpose flour

Instructions

Preheat oven to 350° F.

In the bowl of your mixer, cream butter and sugar until smooth, at least 3 minutes.

Beat in vanilla extract and egg.

In a separate bowl, combine baking powder and salt with flour, and add a little bit at a time to the wet ingredients.

If your dough looks crumbly, keep mixing (another 30 seconds to 1 minute). After that, if it's still a little crumbly, turn the dough out onto a floured surface, wet your hands, and knead it by hand until it is a ball.

Don't chill the dough – it's ready to go! Divide it into three smaller batches and roll out onto a floured surface. When rolling, ¼" thickness (or a little under) is just right.

Cut with your favorite cookie cutters, and put them onto cookie sheets.

Bake at 350 for 8-10 minutes. Let cool on the cookie sheet until firm enough to transfer to a cooling rack.

Once the cookies are cool, decorate with your favorite icing (and sprinkles!). Everything from sugar cookie icing to buttercream to royal icing tastes yummy with these cookies!

What do you do when a child gets caught up in the enthusiasm for gift-giving, and they come up with a long list of items that they want, including a request for a pony?

I've seen lots of very long lists in my time, and what I like to do is to ask the child, "Are there one or two things that are very special on this list? This is a wonderful and creative list. It is important that Santa and I make sure that there is room on the sleigh for everyone to get things that are special to them. Can you help us be sure we have room for everyone?"

When it comes to animals, Santa and I know that pets are a whole-family decision. Everyone needs to be ready to help take care of the animal, and once your family says they're ready, we're happy to bring things like food and water bowls, leashes, and pet toys to help you on your way.

FINAL THOUGHTS

Dear Reader, it is now time for you to write a letter to me. Turn to a blank page in your journal or choose a piece of stationery that delights you. Share your thoughts and your questions. Here are two questions that can be used to spark your creativity:

What do you wish for most of all?

What needs to change for this to happen and for your wish to come true?

This may be the first time you have written to Mrs. Claus, and it may have been years since you wrote a Christmas wish list. Now is your opportunity to do so, and to identify what you hope and wish the future holds just for you. Take a moment to sit quietly and listen to the call to action.

What is it that the world is asking of you now?

Merry always, Mrs. Claus

I am deeply honored by the individuals who take on my persona and share my values as Mrs. Claus presenters and performers. It takes a special person to do this work, and I applaud each one of them. I have read of their years, sometimes decades, of service. These generous and kind-hearted individuals fulfill the important work of uplifting, encouraging, and inspiring all that they meet. Even brief encounters with Mrs. Claus can leave a lasting, positive impact due to the care and attention she gives to each person.

Mrs. Claus performers make appearances with Santa and on their own at schools, churches, hospitals, hospices, parades, charitable events, libraries, hotels, retail stores, municipal and state events, tea parties, cookie-making workshops, and art and craft studios. They make special home visits, have appeared in films, plays, and shows, and have given interviews in the media and on podcasts. They are terrific role models for young children, modeling love and kindness in spectacular fashion. They also do the important work of role modeling teamwork, a loving and successful marriage, and partnership. Mrs. Claus' performance trainings are offered around the United States. These in-person or online programs provide instruction on how to embody the character and master the art of captivating audiences of all ages.

"There is a Mrs. Claus in your neighborhood, wherever you live. I hope you get to meet her someday! Please thank her for me when you do!"

- Mrs. Claus

I invite you to join me each night as I say good night to the moon. I say good night to the moon, and use it as a moment to I think of all the individuals of the past and present, and applaud how they have made the world a kinder and more compassionate place. You share the moon with me as well. When you say good night to the moon, honor all who have gone before you or who supported your efforts on this day. Consider your own legacy, and how the world will be left a better place because you shared your gifts, love, and laughter. Your gestures and words of kindness last throughout the ages. Future generations who say good night to the moon will honor you, as well.

"Listen and look for the word 'joy' during your day. Use the word during a conversation or express it in correspondence. You will be amazed how much joy abounds all around you. Make your own contribution – spread joy."

- Mrs. Claus

Publisher's Page:

Library and Archives Canada Cataloguing in Publication Title: What would Mrs. Claus Do? Where there is a wish, there is a way / written by Pamela McColl and Lindsay Stewart. Names: McColl, Pamela, 1958- author | Stewart, Lindsay, author. Description: Includes index. Identifiers: Canadiana 20250138069 | ISBN 9781927979402 (hardcover) Subjects: LCSH: Claus, Mrs. (Fictitious character) | LCSH: Christmas—Miscellanea. | LCSH: Women— Conduct of life. | LCSH: Women—Life skills guides. | LCGFT: Gift books. Classification: LCC GT4992 .M325 2025 | DDC 394.2663—dc23

First Edition Copyright © 2025 Pamela McColl and Lindsay Stewart. Individual copyrights rest with the authors, photographers, and illustrators. All rights reserved. No part of this publication may be used, reproduced, stored, or introduced into a retrieval system, or transmitted in any form, or by any means, without prior written permission of the publisher. Brief passages and poems may be quoted in reviews or scholarly articles.

Cover photography credit: LKN Images, Cole Eveson. Reprinted with permission.

Photography credit: Lindsay Stewart

Printed by Sung in America, Korea.

Illustration credit: Stock Adobe: 3850392296, 3838228120, 180094759.

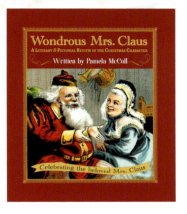

Visit Facebook: Mrs. Claus Book Club to contact the authors or through the publisher's website: www.twasthenightbook.com

Grafton and Scratch Publisher's Christmas titles:

Wondrous Mrs. Claus: A Literary and Pictorial History of the Classic Christmas Character by Pamela McColl (2025) ISBN: 9781927979389.

Twas The Night: The Art and History of the Classic Christmas Poem by Pamela McColl (2023): ISBN 9781927979303.

Twas The Night Before Christmas. A Bicentennial Edition of the Classic Christmas Poem by Clement C. Moore: ISBN 9781927979341.

Board book edition for babies and toddlers: ISBN 9781927979334.

Era la Vispera (Spanish edition): ISBN 9780987902351.

The Boy Who Lived in Pudding Lane by Sarah Addington (1922), reprinted and redesigned (2018): ISBN 9781927979266.